THE YEAR-ROUND
VEGETABLE GARDENER

THE YEAR-ROUND VEGETABLE GARDENER

How to Grow Your Own Food
365 DAYS A YEAR
No Matter Where You Live

Niki Jabbour

Photography by Joseph De Sciose

Storey Publishing

The mission of Storey Publishing is to serve our customers by
publishing practical information that encourages
personal independence in harmony with the environment.

Edited by Carleen Madigan
Art direction and book design by Cynthia N. McFarland
Text production by Liseann Karandisecky and Theresa E. Wiscovitch

Cover and interior photography by © Joseph De Sciose, except for Raylene
    Sampson: back cover, author photo; © Niki Jabbour: 17, 30, 31, 38 bottom, 40,
    43 top and bottom left, 51 bottom, 56 left, 62 left, 64 left, 78, 85, 99, 103 bottom,
    107 bottom, 108 bottom, 114, 132, 140, 142, 151, 153, 158 top center, top right,
    middle, and bottom left, 166, 167, 178, 183, 205 top, 207 top, 210, 212, 215, and
    224 bottom; © Thomas Generazio: 71, 75, 80, 86, and 203; © Brenda Franklin:
    116 right and 117; © Jonathan Buckley: 162 and 163; © Dorling Kindersley/
    Getty Images: 164; © FogStock/Alamy: 135; © Image DJ/agefotostock: 222 top;
    © MIXA/Getty Images: 199
Illustrations by © Elara Tanguy

Indexed by Christine R. Lindemer, Boston Road Communications

© 2011 by Niki Jabbour

Storey Publishing
210 MASS MoCA Way
North Adams, MA 01247
www.storey.com

Printed in China by Toppan Leefung Printing Ltd.
10 9 8 7 6 5 4 3 2 1

LIBRARY OF CONGRESS CATALOGING-IN-PUBLICATION DATA
Jabbour, Niki.
  The year-round vegetable gardener / by Niki Jabbour.
    p. cm.
  Includes index.
  ISBN 978-1-60342-568-1 (pbk. : alk. paper)
  ISBN 978-1-60342-992-4 (hardcover : alk. paper)
  1. Vegetable gardening. I. Title.
SB321.J33 2012
635—dc23
                                        2011024854

CONTENTS

To Dany, Alex, and Isabelle,
my favorite garden helpers!

To my parents, sisters, and in-laws.
Thank you all for your continual sup-
port, encouragement, and willingness
to be garden guinea pigs for a wide
variety of crazy veggies.

ACKNOWLEDGMENTS

I'd like to offer a big thank-you to everyone who made this book possible. I especially appreciate the hard work of my editor, Carleen Madigan, for the endless guidance and advice, as well as her ability to find the humor in any situation. I'm also grateful to the photographer for the book, Joseph De Sciose, who can spot beauty in any scene — from a pile of compost to a pesky slug.

I'd also like to thank the talented team at Storey Publishing for their kind welcome and hard work — art director Cindy McFarland, creative director Alethea Morrison, illustration coordinator Ilona Sherratt, and illustrator Elara Tanguy.

Last, but certainly not least, I owe a huge thank-you to all the gardeners who welcomed Carleen, Joe, and me into their gorgeous gardens: Rob and Brenda Franklin, Duff and Donna Evers, Yvon and Faye Brunet, Barry Dorey and Raylene Sampson, Alan and Darlene Soulsby, Larry and Peggy Brewster, George and Carol Knowles, Robert Cervelli and Susan Williams, John and Judy Risley, Peter Watson, Stephen and Sheila Archibald, Jean Snow and Bob Kropla, Thomas Generazio, Owen Bridge at Annapolis Seeds, and Windhorse Farm.

Foreword

by Roger Doiron

Gardens, like other good ideas, have a way of growing in the most unlikely places. My first vegetable garden sprouted in my imagination while I was living on the top floor of an apartment building in Brussels, Belgium. Five stories up and with no land to call my own, I began planting the seeds of a new homegrown life by reading *Living the Good Life*, Helen and Scott Nearings' back-to-the-land bible about homesteading on the coast of Maine.

The book helped me reconnect with my Maine roots, and with roots in general. But more than that, it helped expand my thinking about what was possible within the generous limits of Maine's climate and soils. And, like a good book should, it also led me to other writers, notably Eliot Coleman, a Maine organic farmer who at the time was quietly redrawing the garden calendar through innovative season extension techniques and structures. Inspired by his experience and the Nearings', I moved back to Maine and grew greens right through a cold and snowy winter.

Now, more than ten years later, the arguments for growing vegetable gardens are stronger than ever, because of mounting concerns about health, climate change, the economy and food security. According to the United Nations' Food and Agriculture Organization, we're going to need to increase global food production by 70 percent over the next 40 years to keep pace with population growth. To meet this challenge, we'll not only need to grow new gardens but also more productive ones.

Fortunately, our knowledge base for how to do this is expanding, thanks to a new crop of gardeners who are pushing the limits of their climates and sharing their findings. Niki Jabbour is an important voice of this new generation of garden writers. She understands — and shares in this helpful new book — that extending the growing season is one of the easiest ways to increase productivity in the garden. We can't invent a new planet, but we can and must learn to use the resources of the current one more creatively, and that includes utilizing the sunshine, warmth, and water that each month offers.

> . . . extending the growing season is one of the easiest ways to increase productivity in the garden. We can't invent a new planet, but we can and must learn to use the resources of the current one more creatively . . .

Whether you're a greenthumb or a greenhorn, I'm sure you'll learn many new things from Niki's experience growing vegetables year-round on the ocean-cooled coast of Nova Scotia. But the most valuable thing this book conveys is a sense of hope and personal empowerment. Although the global challenges we face are formidable, so are our resources. The good life is closer than we may think; we just need to know where and when to start digging, as well as when not to stop.

Roger Doiron is founder of Kitchen Gardeners International, a Maine-based nonprofit network of more than 20,000 individuals from 100 countries who are growing some of their own food and helping others to do the same. He eats year-round from his own garden on the coast of Maine.

JUNE 6

AUGUST 5

Four Seasons of Fresh Vegetables

OCTOBER 14

JANUARY 15

Introduction

It all started with a row cover. Years ago, on an unexpectedly mild day in late November, I happened to wander over to the empty vegetable patch. I hadn't actually been to the garden since the garlic was planted in mid-October, thinking the season was over until the following spring. Yet as I strolled the pathways, I discovered that the bed where we had enjoyed arugula until early October was still going strong! I immediately headed back to the house for a bowl and then returned to pick a big salad for supper.

That night it snowed a few inches, but the next day, I went back up to the garden to see if the arugula had succumbed. It hadn't! Instead, the vigorous leaves were poking out of the snow, begging to be picked. I grabbed a few row covers from the garage that I typically used to protect the tomatoes after spring planting and placed them on top of the arugula patch. With that simple level of protection, we enjoyed arugula from the garden until after Christmas.

I soon began to experiment with some of the hardier vegetables that I found listed in seed catalogs — leeks, salad greens, carrots, scallions, kale — and realized that with some basic shelter, the traditional gardening season could be extended by months. A few good books, such as *Four-Season Harvest* by Eliot Coleman and *Solar Gardening* by Leandre Poisson and Gretchen Vogel Poisson, helped point the way and introduced me to cold-tolerant veggies that I had never heard of before, much less eaten. These included mâche, claytonia, tatsoi, and more.

I also discovered that cold-season gardening involves much less maintenance than does warm-season gardening. Once the temperature plunges in late autumn, little work is needed to keep crops happy. You don't have to water, fight bugs (okay, maybe I find an occasional slug hiding in the cold frames in late autumn), or weed. I think of our winter cold frames as in-ground refrigerators that protect and hold our crops until we're ready to eat them.

As I learned during that first winter, even the most basic season extender — the row cover — can be a valuable tool.

> Even in the dead of winter, we're able to harvest vegetables.

We use our row covers in spring, fall, and winter to protect a wide variety of cool- and cold-season crops. They're even draped over winter carrot and parsnip beds to hold down the thick mulch of shredded leaves that insulates the root crops.

Another handy season-extending tool is the cloche. Gardeners have been using cloches for centuries to shelter crops. What could be easier than putting an old glass jar upside down over a newly planted tomato seedling? Or a milk jug with the bottom removed? Yet this simple barrier against the elements can help expand your growing season by several weeks at either end. I also like the water-filled cloches, which let me plant tomatoes in the garden weeks before the last frost, giving me the earliest tomatoes on the street!

Of course, we don't harvest heirloom tomatoes in January (although I do keep a dozen large bags of garden tomatoes tucked away in the freezer for a winter treat). Rather, we've learned to work with the seasons and grow the right vegetables at the right time. In spring and summer, we have all the usual characters — beans, peas, tomatoes, carrots, broccoli, lettuce, and much, much more. Come autumn, we don't hang up our gloves and put the garden to bed. Instead, we switch gears and begin to harvest the cool-weather vegetables like kale, leeks, scallions, carrots, parsnips, tatsoi, spinach, arugula, and claytonia. Even in the dead of winter, we're able to harvest the most cold-tolerant varieties of these vegetables with the help of season-extending devices like cold frames and mini hoop tunnels. And we don't live in a sunny corner of the world, either. Our garden is perched on the edge of the Atlantic Ocean in the Great White North — Nova Scotia, Canada.

In this book, I'll walk you through the process of creating a year-round vegetable garden. But it's only fair to warn you that the ability to harvest fresh, organic vegetables year-round from your own garden is potentially addictive. It's extremely satisfying, though, and easier than you might think. Interested? Keep reading.

PART 1

Stretching the Seasons

Getting the Timing Right

A**S THE OLD SAYING GOES,** timing is everything. When it comes to year-round vegetable gardening, timing is essential. Not only is it important to time plantings so that each crop is able to grow in its preferred season, but it's also smart to time successive plantings of crops so that you can enjoy a continuous harvest during the growing season.

Our first seeding of the year is timed for late winter, 6 to 8 weeks after the winter solstice, when the day length is steadily increasing and temperatures have started to inch upward. At this point, any empty spaces in our season extenders are sown with a mix of hardy crops like spinach, mâche, Swiss chard, beets, and carrots.

As the weeks pass and the days continue to grow warmer, we sow additional plantings of these vegetables in the open garden beds. If I've played my cards right and Mother Nature cooperates, the late-winter vegetables that I sowed in the cold frames and mini hoop tunnels are just coming into harvest as the first seeds are planted in the unprotected garden.

In early summer, the garden is a flurry of activity as we sow and transplant fresh crops every week to ensure a nonstop harvest of our favorite vegetables.

By late summer, our garden beds and season extenders are once again filled with hardy vegetables for a late-fall and winter harvest. These cool- and cold-tolerant crops need to be timed so that they reach harvestable size before the day length drops to less than 10 hours a day and growth slows dramatically.

This chapter will guide you through the process of timing your year-round vegetable garden, as well as help you take the guesswork out of succession planting and intercropping — two easy techniques that also depend on proper timing.

The Three Growing Seasons

You might think that there is only one growing season. In fact, there are three — cool, warm, and cold. Each season has a range of vegetables that thrive in its climatic conditions; there is some overlap between the seasons, most often with the cool-season veggies, which are very adaptable.

Any vegetable can be grown in a year-round garden, but the real secret to success is matching vegetables with the time of year when they grow best. After all, you wouldn't grow heat-loving veggies like tomatoes in a fall or winter garden. Instead, you'd plant cool- and cold-weather crops like arugula, carrots, leeks, and mâche. By working with the seasons, you'll be able to plan for a nonstop harvest all year long.

> Fall and winter crops of carrots, beets, turnips, and Swiss chard are direct-sown in the garden in mid- to late summer.

Cool Seasons

Spring and autumn are the cool seasons in the garden, times when many traditional vegetable gardeners are flipping through seed catalogs or hanging up their gardening gloves for the season. I love growing in the cool seasons; it's not too hot to work in the garden, few pests threaten emerging crops (besides the ever-present deer and slugs), and a large selection of delicious vegetables thrives in the brisk temperatures of spring and fall.

A cool-season vegetable is simply one that grows best when the air and soil temperatures are cool. Ideal air temperatures for these versatile vegetables range between 40 and 70°F (5–20°C). Once the heat of summer arrives, many of these crops either stop growing or bolt (go to seed), so it's best if you try to time their entire life span so that it falls within the cool season.

Planning ahead. Because many of these vegetables like to be planted so early in the spring, it makes sense to get the garden ready in the fall. As autumn crops are harvested and while the soil is easy to work, I incorporate amendments like compost, aged manure, shredded leaves, and lime. Come spring, wet weather, cold snaps, and frozen compost can make working the soil a chore rather than a pleasure.

Spring sowing. If you planned ahead and prepared the garden the previous autumn, planting cool-season crops in early spring is quick and easy; I typically get the first seeds in the unprotected (or open) garden as soon as the snow has melted, in mid- to late March. Once they're planted, you can help accelerate their growth with a few simple season extenders — row covers, tunnels, and cold frames (see chapter 3, starting on page 36, for more information) — but don't mollycoddle the young plants, as most cool-season crops can easily withstand a light frost.

Although many cool-season vegetables are direct-seeded in the garden, certain crops grow best when they're started indoors and then transplanted. In my garden, I transplant broccoli, cauliflower, cabbage, and leeks, for example. Although I can produce a

Most cool-season crops can be planted as soon as the soil can be worked in early spring.

COOL-SEASON HARVEST

These are some of the vegetables that thrive in the cool spring and fall weather. Many of them, like carrots and Swiss chard, are four-season vegetables that will overwinter with some protection. We use cold frames and mini hoop tunnels to get a jump on the cool season, and start seeds weeks before most gardeners even think of breaking ground.

KALE

SWISS CHARD

LETTUCE

CHIVES

PURPLE PAK CHOI

OVERWINTERED LEEKS

MÂCHE

ASPARAGUS

CARROTS

RADISHES

LETTUCE

decent crop when I direct-seed broccoli, I've found that the heads on the transplanted crops are at least twice as large as those that were direct-seeded. The small size is often due to unreliable early-spring weather as well as the voracious slugs that tend to attack my tiny, newly sprouted broccoli seedlings.

Cool-season vegetables are also ideal for cold-frame culture. My first direct sowings of beets, kohlrabi, carrots, endive, scallions, pak choi, and even seed potatoes are usually planted in the cold frame in late winter (late February to late March).

Surviving summer. Once late spring starts to sprint toward summer, the cool-season vegetables begin to sulk with the increasing daylight and heat. At this point, it's time to start switching to warm-season crops such as beans, tomatoes, peppers, basil, and

Cool Roots and Hot Fruits

Did you know that the season in which a crop is grown can also indicate which parts of the plant we eat? Cool and cold season crops are typically grown for their roots, stems, leaves, or immature flowers — radishes, carrots, lettuce, spinach, and broccoli, for example. With warm season crops, we usually consume the immature or mature fruits, like tomatoes, peppers, cucumbers, and beans. The exceptions to the rule are peas and broad beans, which are cool season crops with edible fruiting parts.

heat-tolerant greens. I do, however, tuck clumps of endive, pak choi, and lettuce under my pole-bean tepees and A-frame trellises, where they'll have some shelter from the sun. You can also use the hoops of your mini tunnels in summer to create a cool bed for these crops by covering the supports with a length of shade cloth. At this time, I also sow another crop of peas for a late-summer and early-autumn harvest.

Another task for early and midsummer is to start more seeds indoors for late-summer and autumn planting. Our grow lights are kept in production from March until August, which provides a continual supply of fresh seedlings for the garden. In early and midsummer, I sow seed for succession and fall crops of cool-season and cold-tolerant veggies like broccoli, kale, kohlrabi, collards, leeks, scallions, endive, and hardy greens. The grow lights are an essential part of our year-round planting schedule and really enable us to maximize our limited space and successfully extend our harvest for the longest possible length of time.

Our carrot cold frame and winter carrot beds are also direct-seeded in midsummer. Because carrot seed and the young seedlings can be a bit finicky, I give them regular drinks and keep a sharp eye out for slugs until they're established. Fall crops of beets, turnips, and Swiss chard are also direct-sown in the garden in mid- to late summer.

Fall planting. In late summer and into autumn, when the temperatures start to drop and the days become shorter, the cool-weather crops are once again the stars of the show. In fact, many cool-weather vegetables grow best in

the autumn and, with a little protection, can be enjoyed well into winter.

By early autumn, the summer-transplanted broccoli, cauliflower, and cabbage, for example, are starting to mature for a late-season feast, while we continue to seed more salad greens directly in the garden. Winter lettuces, claytonia, mâche, arugula, mustard, and spinach, along with quick-growing root vegetables like radishes and baby beets, are planted in the cold frames, as well as in the open garden, where they will eventually be covered with row covers or mini hoop tunnels. Late summer–started transplants of endive, Chinese cabbage, escarole, and scallions are also moved into the garden or cold frames in early autumn, where they will be enjoyed for several months.

Warm Season

Warm-season vegetables are in their glory in the bright summer sun. Unlike cool-season crops, they don't tolerate frost. Unless you're using a cold frame, a row cover, or another protective structure, warm-season crops shouldn't be planted into the garden until late spring, when all risk of frost has passed.

Spring sowing. Crops can be quick growing, like bush beans and New Zealand spinach, or they might be long-season crops like sweet potatoes, melons, tomatoes, and eggplant. The long-season types are generally started indoors or purchased as transplants; the quick-growing crops can be direct-seeded in the garden.

Although they're considered relatively quick to grow from seed and are often seeded directly in the garden, I like to start my cucumbers, squash, and pumpkins indoors 4 to 6 weeks

WARM-SEASON HARVEST

These are the boys of summer — the vegetables that need warmth and lots of sunlight in order to thrive. Most warm-season crops are tender and will die with just the slightest frost, but selecting short-season varieties and using the protection of season extenders will help ensure a bumper crop. Many cool-season vegetables — carrots, beets, cabbage, and salad greens, are extremely adaptable and if planted while the weather is still cool can also be harvested in summer.

MUSTARD

BASIL

NASTURTIUMS

CABBAGE

CUCUMBER

ONIONS

SAGE

EGGPLANT

CAULIFLOWER

SUMMER SQUASH

POLE BEANS

TOMATOES

before the last spring frost. It may not be necessary to ensure a crop, but because our springs can be unpredictable, I find this timing gives me a good head start on some of our favorite warm-season vegetables. Other long-maturing warm-season vegetables, like tomatoes and peppers, need a good 8- to 10-week start before they're large enough to be transplanted into the garden.

Planting out. Warm-season crops need both warm soil and warm air temperatures in order to germinate and grow well. Most gardeners wait to plant until mid-spring when soil and air temperatures have warmed up to at least 50°F (10°C). You can, however, plant a few weeks earlier if you warm up the soil first and protect a crop once it's planted.

To warm the soil, lay a sheet of black plastic over the garden bed a week or two prior to planting. After the soil has warmed, some gardeners leave the black plastic in place and plant directly into it by cutting holes

and poking the seedlings through the openings. This helps lock in soil heat and moisture, as well as discourages weeds — always a good thing. It also reduces the spread of blight, which is caused by water splashing soil up onto the plants.

The downside is that it can be difficult to water the plants once the summer heat sets in, and if the soil warms up too much, certain crops, like tomatoes and peppers, may experience blossom drop. Because of this, I remove the black plastic once the soil has warmed up, in mid- to late spring, and then plant the bed with my tomato seedlings 3 or 4 weeks earlier than usual. I then cover each tomato plant with a cloche or a water-filled cloche (see Water-Filled Cloches, page 44).

For a quick tomato cloche, insert a metal tomato cage over the newly planted seedling and wrap it with a clear plastic sheet, leaving the top open for ventilation. Use clothespins or binder clips to secure the plastic. Alternatively, if you're planting your tomatoes (or eggplants, or peppers, or zucchini) in rows or long beds, cover the seedlings with a temporary mini hoop tunnel until the risk of frost has passed (see page 60 for more about mini hoop tunnels).

Choosing the right varieties. Often, gardeners in cold climates shy away from warm-season crops like tomatoes and peppers. Yet with a little planning, and some season extenders, even short-season gardeners can enjoy a bounty of vine-ripened tomatoes. Combining these extenders with proper plant selection will boost success even further. Start by choosing short-season, quick-maturing varieties. For example, 'Moskvich' and 'Sub

Arctic Maxi' tomatoes are extra-early-maturing varieties that are ready about 60 days after transplanting and are a better choice for cold-climate gardeners than Brandywine, for example, which can take up to 80 days to ripen.

Cold Season

Cold-season crops are a year-round gardener's best friend. These are the vegetables that will help you get through the long, dark winter, when most other gardeners are simply reading seed catalogs and dreaming about spring. There is nothing the summer garden can offer that is as invigorating as lifting a cold frame lid on a frosty January afternoon to pick some hardy greens for a gourmet winter salad.

The winter garden is also full of hidden treasures — think of carrot, parsnip, and celeriac roots tucked beneath a thick layer of straw just waiting for you to dig them out and taste their unbelievable sweetness. The leafy shoots of hardy kale and collards will perk up winter cooking and add a nutritional punch, as well.

Fall prep work. To simplify late-winter planting, prepare your garden beds the previous autumn — as you would for cool-season crops. Once fall crops have been harvested, any areas that are to be left unplanted during the winter should be amended with manure or compost or planted with a cover crop.

Even if you aren't covering existing vegetables with a mini hoop tunnel, fall is a great time to set your hoops for a spring hoop planting. If you wait until spring, the ground may still be frozen when you're ready to plant your cold-season crops. Putting up the supports in the fall is quick and easy. Then, once early spring rolls

Long after all the other vegetable gardeners in your neighborhood have put their plots to bed for the winter, you'll still be harvesting fresh greens and sweet root vegetables from your cold frames and mini hoop tunnels. These cold-tolerant vegetables can also be grown in the cool seasons of spring and autumn.

BRUSSELS SPROUTS

PARSLEY

LEEKS

KALE

LETTUCE

PARSNIPS

SCALLIONS

MÂCHE

SPINACH

CARROTS

BEETS

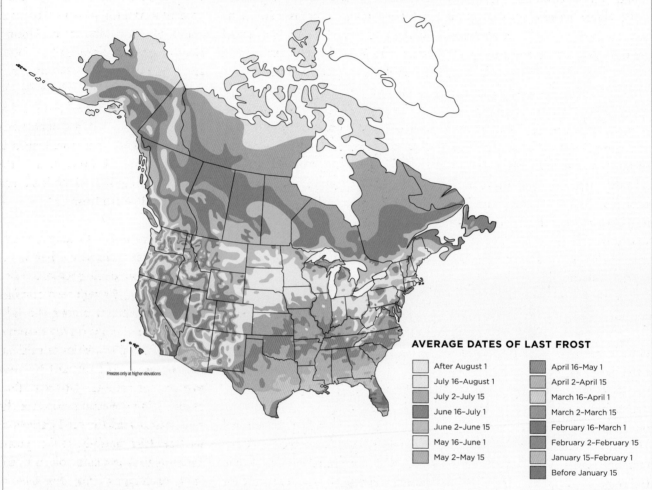

Freezes only at higher elevations

AVERAGE DATES OF LAST FROST

After August 1	April 16–May 1
July 16–August 1	April 2–April 15
July 2–July 15	March 16–April 1
June 16–July 1	March 2–March 15
June 2–June 15	February 16–March 1
May 16–June 1	February 2–February 15
May 2–May 15	January 15–February 1
	Before January 15

TO BE A SUCCESSFUL year-round vegetable gardener, you'll need to know the length and average dates of the frost-free season for your region. Knowing the frost dates is the key to setting a planting schedule for a nonstop harvest. If you don't know the approximate dates for the last spring frost and first fall frost in your immediate area, ask an experienced gardening friend, the experts at a nearby garden center, or an agent from your local Cooperative Extension Service. The information can also be found online (follow the link in Resources, page 236).

Keep in mind that the dates for the last spring and first fall frosts are approximate, not written in stone. The last spring frost in my area is usually in mid-May, but I've gardened long enough to know that a late frost is not only possible, but also likely. In fact, it seems that I can generally expect a frost the day after I plant my tomatoes into the open garden. Because of this shifting frost date, I keep handy a supply of row covers to protect newly transplanted tomatoes, peppers, cucumbers, and other tender vegetables from late-spring frosts. It also helps to listen to the local weather forecast around the average frost dates to ensure that a late-spring or early-autumn frost won't take you (and your tomatoes) by surprise.

Although cool- and cold-season crops can be grown outside of this frost-free window between the last spring and first autumn frost, the warm-season crops need to be planted, grow, and produce their bounty between its borders (with a bit of leeway at either end of the season when you're using season extenders like mini hoop tunnels).

And even though the hardier crops can withstand frost, you'll still need to know your frost dates to help you plan your planting schedule. For example, in order to ensure a bumper crop of winter carrots, I know that I need to sow the seed 8 to 10 weeks before the first fall frost — early to mid-August in my region.

around, you can cover the hoops with plastic about a week or two before you're ready to plant. This shelter will give the soil a chance to warm up.

Late-winter sowing. Cold-season vegetables are the first crops that can be planted in the late-winter and early-spring garden. We sow arugula, mustard, tatsoi, spinach, hardy lettuce, and other greens in any empty areas of the cold frames starting in mid- to late February, as well as sprinkle the same seed in the garden under the protective covering of the now mostly empty hoop tunnels.

To plant in a mini hoop tunnel, lift one side of the plastic, sowing your seeds on the soil surface and labeling before lowering and securing the side of the tunnel. Vent the ends on mild and warm days, and before you know it, you'll be tucking into a big bowl of gourmet winter greens.

In the darkest parts of winter, when the garden receives less than 10 hours of sunlight per day, the fall-planted cold-season vegetable plants in the cold frame may not be actively growing, but they'll continue to be harvestable. This is true even though they will experience freezing temperatures. Pop open the top of a cold frame on a frosty morning, and it looks as though all the plants have been turned into veggie popsicles! At this point, most crops cannot be harvested without turning into a pile of mush. Yet within a few hours, the weak winter sun will have warmed up the interior of the frame enough that the temperature has risen above freezing and you can harvest the now defrosted vegetables. Even a cloudy day in winter will usually warm up the frames enough that we can harvest by late morning and into mid-afternoon.

Fall sowing. Cold-season vegetables are frost-tolerant crops and many of them can stand in the garden all winter long with little protection, especially in regions with mild winters (Zones 6+). For a successful winter harvest, you need to time your cold-season crops properly. Although they will continue to grow, albeit at a slower pace as the nights turn chilly, the majority of their growth will take place when the weather is still warm — in late summer and early autumn — and while there is still more than 10 hours of sunlight per day. Cold-season crops should be almost mature by the time the cold weather finally arrives, in late autumn. The vegetables will then hold in the garden all winter long — typically under a simple season extender like a cold frame or a tunnel.

Timing. To successfully time your fall and winter crops, you need to know two pieces of information — the average date of the first fall frost for your region and the days to maturity for the vegetable you're planting.

For example, if my average first frost date is October 20 and I want to grow a late-autumn crop of broccoli, I would first choose a cold-tolerant type like Marathon, which matures about 68 days after transplanting. Because growth slows in the cooler and waning-light days of autumn, I would add an extra week or two to the days to maturity and assume that my crop would be ready about 80 days from transplant. Therefore, I need to transplant my fall broccoli into the garden on August 1, which is 80 days before my first fall frost.

Choosing cultivars. Picking the right variety is essential and another way to stretch your gardening season. When you're flipping through seed catalogs, remember that even among the individual types of crops (in my example, broccoli), certain varieties or cultivars may be more cold tolerant (or heat tolerant for summer growing) than others. When selecting crops for the cold season, read the seed packets or seed catalogs carefully, so that you're choosing the most cold-tolerant variety of each type of crop. For a list of the best varieties of each crop for the different growing seasons, check out Niki's Picks, which are listed after each vegetable description in part 2 (beginning on page 96).

Many cool-season crops can be harvested well into winter with a simple season extender like this homemade mini hoop tunnel.

Considering Day Length and Growing Seasons

Temperature isn't the only factor to consider when planting a year-round vegetable garden; it's also important to understand how changing levels of sunlight affect plant growth. As summer races into fall, the day length begins to shorten and there is less available light. Because most fall and winter crops are planted in late summer and early autumn, their initial growth will be quick, but as the days shorten and the temperature drops, growth will start to slow down.

Therefore, it's important to time your fall and winter crops carefully. Ideally, your cold-weather vegetables should be almost mature (about 90 percent grown) by the time the day length falls to less than 10 hours per day. At that point, most active growth will stop and your vegetables will then hold under their season extenders (cold frames, tunnels, etc.) until you're ready to harvest. It's not difficult; it just takes a bit of planning to time your crops properly. And to figure out the timing, you need to find the answers to the following four important questions.

What is the length of your growing season?

In North America, the growing season is usually considered to be the length of time between the last spring frost and the first autumn frost. My season is approximately 120 days, but that can vary by a week or two at the beginning or end of the season from one year to the next.

To find out the approximate length of your growing season, contact your local agricultural bureau or Cooperative Extension Service, or ask a knowledgeable gardener in your neighborhood. (You can go online to find the Cooperative Extension branch nearest you; follow the link on page 236.) This information is your guide to choosing the right crops for your garden, as well as helping you figure out what succession crops will have enough time to mature before the first autumn frost arrives.

Certain vegetables, like leaf lettuce and radishes, are very quick growing and will have plenty of time to mature in most regions. Others, such as sweet potatoes, need a very long, warm growing season. Since I know that my season is often too short to count on a sweet potato harvest, I choose other crops.

> Cold-weather vegetables should be almost mature (about 90 percent grown) by the time the day length falls to less than 10 hours per day.

What do you want to grow?

When you're planning the timing of your crops, you'll also need to make a list of your desired vegetables, which will help you match each crop with its ideal season of growth.

Once the seed catalogs start to arrive in December (I end up with about 30 catalogs by the time spring finally rolls around), I begin jotting down a wish list for the upcoming year. My list is pretty extensive and contains both family favorites and new crops to try. In particular, I'm always on the lookout for more winter-hardy crops to add to the cold-season garden. Don't be afraid to experiment with new vegetables or different varieties of common crops like pole beans and peas. You may discover a new favorite, or one that is more cold tolerant than what you've been growing for years. Next to each item on my list of vegetables, I pencil in the ideal growing season. This keeps me organized and enables me to plan when each crop needs to be grown.

How long will it take for these vegetables to mature?

Most cool- and cold-season crops can be grown, or at least harvested, for a large portion of the year, whereas warm-season crops need to be grown in the traditional season between the spring and fall frosts. The seed packet or catalog lists the "days to maturity" for each crop, so you can calculate whether your season is long enough to allow adequate time for the crop to mature. Read this information carefully, as it can be listed as "days to maturity from seed" or "days to maturity from transplant."

Don't despair if you feel limited by living in a cold climate. Even if your season is too short for certain long- or warm-season crops, by using or combining the season extenders described in chapter 3 (beginning on page 34), you can create microclimates within your garden that will enable you to stretch your season and grow a wider variety of crops.

As the day length shortens in late summer, plant growth slows down. Therefore, when planting for a fall and winter harvest, add an extra week or two to the "days to maturity" listed for your crops, to allow them enough time to mature before the onset of winter.

A Year in the Life of
My Grow Lights

LATE WINTER

Once February rolls around and my seed orders have begun to arrive, I know that it's time to think about seed starting. I head down to the basement, where I have four 48-inch grow lights set up permanently, and give them a good wipe-down, removing any dust or debris from last season. If the bulbs need to be changed, I insert new ones and recycle the old ones.

My earliest seedings are hardy, spring-planted crops: celery, leeks, broccoli, cabbage, kale, mustard, endive, and green onions. I'll sow the seed in mid-February and place the flats under one of the grow lights. Sometimes I'll even start tender vegetables, like 'Imperial Star' artichokes, in early February for a midsummer treat! They're not cold hardy, but by planting them indoors early and then giving them a taste of cool temperatures for a few weeks, I can trick them into thinking they've undergone a winter, and they'll produce a respectable crop.

Once the Ides of March arrive, I know it's time to start seeding the majority of my spring-planted vegetables: tomatoes, peppers, lettuces (at least a dozen types!), fennel, and Italian parsley; Asian vegetables; and more of the brassicas, like broccoli, Brussels sprouts, cabbage, and kohlrabi. I take great pleasure digging out my supplies — seeding trays, plug flats, cell packs, plant tags, and potting soil — to get ready for the seeding rush. Even the kids like to help. Most crops are started by mid-March and soon space becomes very tight under the grow lights. In early April, it's time to seed several varieties of cucumber and zucchini.

◄ Like many other gardeners, I start seedlings for my summer garden under grow lights in early spring. The same lights can be used to grow salad greens indoors through the winter.

▶ When the summer harvest is rolling in, I'm still using my grow lights to start seedlings for fall and winter harvest.

SPRING

By the time mid-May rolls around, most of the seedlings have been hardened off and tucked into the garden. At this point, many gardeners put away their seed-starting equipment and turn off their lights until the next year, but as a year-round vegetable gardener, I know that my trusty grow lights are an easy way to keep the garden in high production through summer, fall, and into winter.

When the last of the spring-planted crops — the heat-loving tomatoes, peppers, cucumbers, and squash — are moved from under the grow lights to harden off, it's time to start thinking about succession crops. Now, most of the cold frame crops have been harvested and anything that grew under the hoop tunnels has long since been picked. Even most of the tunnels themselves have been put away for the summer, except those that will offer a little early protection to the warm-season crops — tomatoes, beans, peppers, corn, and squash.

By May's end, the early-seeded lettuces and assorted salad greens are in their full glory, providing daily bowls of green, red, bronze, and speckled leaves. In order to keep production high, I'll sprinkle more lettuce, arugula, and spinach seeds in any empty areas of the garden, but I'll also start more under the grow lights. When the weather heats up in June, I find it easier to seed certain succession crops indoors rather than trying to coax cool-season crops like lettuce to germinate in the heat. I'm also not fond of watering newly seeded beds frequently, and starting flats of salad greens indoors lets me keep garden watering to a minimum. Typically, I always have a few flats of new seedlings coming along and a few outdoors in a shaded spot being hardened off for transplanting.

SUMMER

In early July, I switch gears and start seeding some fall crops — kale, hardy broccoli, cabbage, kohlrabi, collards, endive, and escarole, under the lights. The basement is much warmer in early July than it was way back in February, and the seeds germinate quickly. I could seed these hardy vegetables directly in the garden, but I worry about slug damage. Also, the seeds of many crops will refuse to germinate once the soil temperature gets up around 85°F (29°C). After about 4 weeks, the young plants are ready to be hardened off and moved into the garden or the open cold frames for fall and winter crops.

FALL

In early August, the first frost is still about 2 months away — give or take a few weeks — and I go back to seeding salad crops for late-summer and autumn harvests. When early September arrives, seed starting for the garden stops, but the lights are still used to nurture a wide variety of herbs — rosemary, basil, and thyme — as well as trays of microgreens for a midwinter treat.

Intensive Planting:
The Key to Nonstop Crops

I N ADDITION TO PLANTING with the seasons and choosing the
right varieties, a nonstop year-round vegetable garden relies
on a variety of intensive-gardening techniques. Intensive gardening is a traditional method developed by French market
farmers in the late 1800s that enabled gardeners to grow more
food in less space. It was based on two main practices — plant-

ing vegetables close together and amending the soil often with compost, aged manure, and other organic materials.

The close spacing, which is usually much tighter than what is recommended on seed packets or in catalogs, creates a living mulch that helps shade out weeds, reduce soil moisture evaporation, and regulate the soil temperature. Growing plants so close together will dramatically increase the amount of food that you can harvest from each bed, but it will require regular applications of aged organic matter in order to keep the level of production high. To maintain fertility in our garden, we add compost or rotted manure between successive crops.

In the following section, I have detailed the two main techniques for successful intensive gardening — succession planting and interplanting.

Soil Building, Year-Round

It's a fact: Healthy soil equals healthy plants, and experienced gardeners know to nourish the soil, not the crop. Maintaining healthy soil, especially when you're planting intensively, isn't difficult but requires a bit of planning. What are the best amendments for the garden? How often do you need to apply them, and when? How do you keep the soil fertile in a high-production, year-round vegetable garden?

Starting in Autumn

Fall is the best time to prepare new garden beds and amend existing ones. If you're starting with poor soil, turning it into dark, loose, loamy soil will take numerous applications of organic matter and a little patience. You can speed things up, however, by combining some basic soil-building techniques — by incorporating aged manure and then planting a cover crop, for example.

In a traditional summer-only garden, horticultural lime is applied to raise soil pH in late autumn, once all the crops have been harvested. In a year-round vegetable garden, it's more difficult to lime all at once, because large portions of the garden are still in production in fall. Lime won't burn or otherwise injure your plants, but it can be difficult for the lime to reach the soil if the beds are still filled with crops. Because of this, I lime any empty beds in mid-November, before the weather turns too cold, picking a calm day just before a rain to minimize the mess. The parts of the garden that are under winter production are left alone and will be limed in the very early spring, after all the winter crops have been harvested.

Spring Feeding

Gardeners with alkaline soil, rather than acid, need to take action in the spring. To lower soil pH, they can amend their garden soil with elemental sulfur. As with lime, results are not instantaneous and make take a few months; incorporating it into the top 6 inches of soil will help speed up the process. Unlike lime, elemental sulfur is best applied in the spring; it needs microbial activity in order to become active.

▶ Producing your own compost from kitchen scraps and garden waste is an easy and inexpensive way to invest in the health of your soil and help maximize the amount of food your garden produces.

Compost or rich, well-composted manure can also be worked into the soil prior to planting in spring, added directly to the planting hole for greedy crops like pumpkins and squash, used as a side-dressing for young plants, or made into a manure tea to offer crops a liquid boost.

With Each Succession

Growing year-round can take its toll on the soil, so an application of compost between successive crops (as well as practicing proper crop rotation) will help prevent nutrient depletion. Heavy feeders like corn may need an additional shot of organic fertilizer throughout the warm season.

Cover Cropping

I often give garden beds and cold frames a break between successive crops by seeding a quick-growing green manure like buckwheat or winter rye (see the box at right). Since our garden has eight large beds (which have been further divided into small planting areas), I like to keep at least one of the main beds planted with a cover crop at all times. This allows most of the garden to be in peak veggie production, but also lets me build up the soil as we harvest bushels of beans, peas, carrots, and salad greens. As crops are harvested and new beds open up, we rotate the green manure bed, so that over the course of a year, each bed has had a chance to be enriched by a cover crop.

Cover crops suppress weeds, improve poor soils, and provide habitat for beneficial insects.

I tend to plant annual green manure crops to avoid any problems that could be caused by the resprouting roots of perennial cover crops. Also, no matter which type of crop you grow, make sure to mow it down or dig it under before the plants go to seed. Otherwise, you'll be introducing a host of new weeds into your garden beds.

Once you've dug under your green manure crop, wait 2 to 3 weeks before you replant the bed. This will give the crop adequate time to break down and release its nutrients back into the soil. You can also sow a quick-growing cover crop between plants a few weeks before you intend to harvest. This will give you a jump on soil building and ensure that the soil isn't left bare for any period of time.

TOP GREEN MANURE CROPS

ALSO KNOWN AS COVER CROPS for their ability to cover the soil and prevent weed growth and erosion, green manure crops are an easy way to build up the health of your soil or quickly improve poor soil. They suppress weeds and stop soil erosion, but they also break up hard, compact soils, protect the surface from the baking rays of the sun, and bring up minerals locked deep underground. Plus, when they are turned under, they add organic matter and nutrients to the soil. They also provide habitat for hardworking soil creatures like worms.

BUCKWHEAT. Buckwheat can be dug under just 6 to 8 weeks after planting. If you let it go to seed, you'll find yourself picking buckwheat babies from your garden beds, so be sure to dig it under before seed heads develop.

WINTER RYE. I generally go through several pounds of winter rye seed each year. It's very quick to grow and can be seeded in fall and dug under in early spring. I also use it to build up the cold frame soil in summer, when the frames are out of production.

ALFALFA. A nitrogen fixer, alfalfa takes nitrogen from the air and makes it available to plants in a form they can use. This helpful trait is also found in other legumes — peas, beans, and clover, for example — which can all be used as green manure crops. Alfalfa is slow to grow, but it has deep roots that will bring up trapped minerals and break up hard soils.

GARDEN PEAS. Another nitrogen-fixing green manure crop, peas can be used to bulk up your soil in spring, summer, or fall. The plants will produce a good supply of organic matter, not to mention a bounty of sweet, juicy peas! When the harvest is over, add the vines to the composter or dig them under.

Gallery of Soil Amendments

KELP

PELLETED LIME

BLOOD MEAL

BONE MEAL

COMPOST

ALFALFA MEAL

AGED MANURE

AS PLANTS GROW, they use up soil nutrients. A gardener's job is to replace those nutrients by feeding the soil with various amendments, cover crops and, if necessary, organic fertilizers. Growing year-round can deplete soil nutrients and organic matter, so it's important to keep on top of the health of your soil. If your garden isn't producing as well as it has in the past, or if you're unsure of the soil's pH and fertility, consider getting a soil test.

PELLETED LIME. If you garden in an area with acid soil, never underestimate the power of lime. Soil that is too sour or too sweet will not be able to make nutrients available to plants. Because the native soil in my region is typically quite acid, we need to give the garden an annual dose of ground horticultural limestone to maintain a relatively neutral pH. Lime also contains calcium, an important nutrient for plant growth.

BONEMEAL. A slow-release source of phosphorus, bone meal is best applied directly to the planting hole, so that fruiting veggies, like tomatoes, have a steady supply of this major nutrient.

ALFALFA MEAL. Alfalfa meal is a renewable resource that comes from alfalfa, a common green manure crop. It contains some major nutrients and is also very high in trace minerals. Alfalfa meal will increase soil organic matter and contains triacontanol, a growth hormone.

KELP. Offered in both liquid and granular forms, this seaweed is a priceless gift to a gardener. Liquid kelp can be used as a foliar spray; kelp meal can be worked into the soil to supply a range of trace nutrients, as well as a dose of plant hormones. Kelp meal can also be used as a compost activator.

BLOOD MEAL. Blood meal is dried, powdered blood that is a good source of nitrogen. It can be worked into the soil or dissolved in water and applied as a liquid fertilizer. Follow package directions carefully to avoid burning your plants. Make sure it is well buried, as animals may find it attractive.

COMPOST. Our compost bins play a central role in the health of our year-round garden. We fill them with garden debris, vegetable peelings, and shredded leaves, and they turn these materials into a dark brown soil amendment that is so prized by gardeners that it's often called black gold.

AGED MANURE. Manure is a great source of organic matter and is available bagged at garden centers or in bulk from local farms. Adding manure to your soil will increase its moisture and nutrient retention, reduce compaction, and improve the overall structure. Keep in mind, though, that the amount of nutrients found in manure will vary widely, depending on the type of animal, the bedding material used for the animal, and how long the manure has been aged.

Succession Planting

The goal of succession planting is simple — to enjoy a continuous and uninterrupted supply of fresh vegetables. This type of planting is particularly important in small backyard gardens, where space is at a premium. Many of my favorite crops for succession planting are those that thrive in the cool and cold weather of spring and fall. They enjoy an extended growing season, unlike the warm season crops, which have a very specific window of cultivation between the frost dates.

Succession planting starts with a little planning. Make a list of what you want to grow, and then write in the expected planting dates and the number of days to harvest. This will tell you how long it will take from the time you plant until you can expect to start harvesting the crop. Because some crops, like leaf lettuce, can produce over an extended period, it's also helpful to know the general length of the expected harvest. Once the crop is finished, it's time to replant. (Check out the handy chart on succession planting, on page 232, to simplify the process.)

In addition to creating an endless harvest, practicing succession planting can help you outwit certain insect pests by avoiding their prime season. For example, if squash vine borers are a problem in your garden, planting a second crop of zucchini in early summer, after the adults have finished laying their eggs, will help ensure that you get to enjoy the fruits of your labor.

To put succession planting to work for you, keep the following tenets in mind.

Succession planting helps ensure a continuous supply of high-quality vegetables. Most salad crops can be sown every few weeks for a nonstop harvest.

Keep on Seeding

One of the easiest ways to practice succession planting is simply to keep on seeding. This technique works best with quick-growing vegetables, like lettuce, arugula, radishes, and bush beans, which can be planted every few weeks. Continual sowing will produce a staggered harvest — that is, your whole crop isn't ready at the same time. After all, who needs to have a whole packet of radish seed mature at once? For a family of four, it makes more sense to sow about 20 radish seeds every 2 weeks. Once radishes reach maturity, they start to lose their quality rather quickly. By planting in succession, you'll be able to harvest perfectly mature radishes for months.

In order to keep on seeding, you'll need to leave space in your garden bed for subsequent plantings. In our garden, a 4-by-4-foot bed is often divided into six mini rows, each measuring about 8 inches wide and planted right up next to each other. No wasted space! I can sow a mini row of leaf lettuce or mesclun mix every 2 weeks for a continuous crop from early spring to late fall. By the time your second and third mini rows are ready to harvest, the first is exhausted and ready for the compost heap. Work an inch of compost into the original row and then replant with more leaf lettuce, or another crop of your choice.

Some crops that are ideal for this type of succession planting are most salad greens, radishes, bush beans, beets, kohlrabi, and carrots.

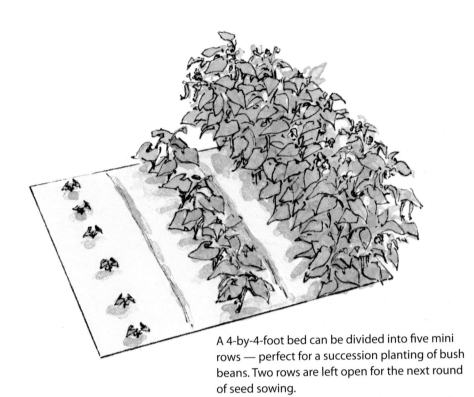

A 4-by-4-foot bed can be divided into five mini rows — perfect for a succession planting of bush beans. Two rows are left open for the next round of seed sowing.

Pick and Sow

I also like to practice the pick-and-sow type of succession planting. This allows me to grow a continuous series of vegetables in the same space over the course of the gardening year by following one crop with another. Once the first crop is finished, I remove it and plant another in its place. For example, I often follow spring radishes with Black Seeded Simpson lettuce, followed by arugula, followed by tomatoes, followed by a crop of fall radishes. The garden space is never empty, and by varying the types of vegetables that are grown in each successive planting, I help

FIVE TIPS FOR SUCCESSFUL SUCCESSION PLANTING

PLAN IN ADVANCE. Although I can't claim to be a super-organized gardener, I'm always sure to order enough seed with my annual orders for a full year of succession planting. A bonus is that, if stored properly, most seed will easily keep for several years, so even if you don't use it all that first season, you can save the rest for the future.

START MORE SEEDLINGS. By mid-May, my warm-season veggie seedlings have been planted in the garden, and the space under my grow light is empty. But it's not time to unplug for the season. Instead, I start planning for succession crops and fall/winter harvests. I start by planting more cucumber seeds, which are relatively quick growing and will supply a second crop of crisp cukes for a late-summer harvest, just when the first crop starts to lose steam. Also, I'll seed more celery for a second yield in late summer and fall. The first planting tends to get pithy and hollow if left to mature. Then, in mid-June, I'll plant a new crop of broccoli and kale that will be transplanted to the garden in late July for a cool- and cold-season harvest. With a little protection, the kale will keep producing throughout the winter.

FEED THE SOIL. To keep production high, I always add a 1-inch layer of compost to the garden between successive crops. If your soil isn't overly fertile, add a granular organic fertilizer at this time; just be sure to follow the directions on the package.

TURN OVER PLANTINGS QUICKLY. To get the most out of your space, remove any spent crops immediately after harvest or as soon as their production declines. Don't wait for the last few peas to mature — just haul out the plants, toss them on the compost pile, and replant right away with another family favorite.

DON'T FORGET ROTATION. Although it's easy to get caught up in the whirlwind of succession planting, it's important to keep in mind what's planted where. A notebook will come in handy! Try to group families (for example, legumes — beans, peas, soybeans). If certain diseases or insects are an annual issue, it is essential to keep rotating your crops. A three-year rotation is considered adequate for most problems, although the longer the rotation, the better. (For more info on crop rotation, see page 82.)

Once quality declines or plants go to seed, pull them and replace with fresh seed or transplants.

Top Five Vegetables for Succession Planting

1 **LEAF LETTUCE.** Because we eat so many salads and because it's so quick and easy to grow, I rely on leaf lettuce to fill in any unexpected empty spaces in the garden. A quick sprinkling of seed results in a generous harvest in just a few weeks. What could be easier? Plus, with such an array of leaf colors, shapes, and textures, lettuces are as pretty as they are productive.

2 **ARUGULA.** Arugula is another workhorse in the garden. It tolerates the unstable weather of early spring and late autumn, and grows so quickly that its nickname is "rocket."

3 **BUSH BEANS.** Bush beans are an ideal veggie for succession planting, as many varieties are ready to harvest in just 50 days. We start sowing seed directly in the garden in mid-May and continue to sow seed every 2 to 3 weeks until late July.

4 **RADISHES.** Perhaps the perfect succession crop, radishes are ridiculously fast growing; they're often ready for harvest in just 21 days. Unless you have a serious hankering for radishes, just sow a small amount of seed every week or two for a continuous supply of fresh roots. You can also succession-plant an assortment of varieties for an extended harvest. We like 'Cherry Belle' (21 days), 'French Breakfast' (28 days), and 'White Icicle' (35 days).

5 **CARROTS.** One of my garden goals is to have fresh carrots ready for harvest 365 days a year! Although that takes both planning and luck, we are able to enjoy carrots most of the year. In spring, summer, and fall, baby carrots are ready to pick in just under 2 months! You can also get a jump on the spring crop by sowing a band of seed in the cold frame in late winter.

prevent the depletion of certain nutrients. Any crop can be grown with this technique, as long as you're planting at a time appropriate to the vegetable (cool, warm, or cold season) and leaving enough time for the crop to mature.

Another easy way to use the pick-and-sow method is to let the season dictate what you'll plant. For example, start with a cool-season crop, like peas or broccoli, that can be planted very early in the spring (super-early crops can be grown under mini hoop tunnels). Once this initial crop has been harvested, the weather will have warmed up and a warm-season crop — corn, tomatoes, or bush beans — can be planted in the same space. After a late-summer harvest, pull the warm-season crop and replace it with another cool- or cold-season vegetable — kale, arugula, winter lettuce, spinach, radishes, or mâche, for example.

Choose Staggered Cultivars

My family loves broccoli, so I like to have an ample supply on hand from early summer to late autumn. Keeping a handful of broccoli transplants on hand for succession planting every few weeks is a pain, though; I'm just not that organized! I rely on the third succession planting technique, choosing staggered cultivars, which enables me to make just two plantings — one in spring for a summer harvest and one in midsummer for a fall harvest. The key is to select varieties that mature at different times, so each harvest, summer and fall, is extended for as long as possible. You can buy separate varieties or you can buy a mixed packet of seed (often called All-Season Blend or something similar). By planting early, mid-, and late-maturing types of broccoli at once, our summer harvest stretches over a period of about 2 months instead of 3 weeks. This mixture of maturity dates prevents all 40 of our broccoli plants from being ready at the same time, which might be fine for a market garden but not for a backyard family vegetable patch. No matter how much we like it, one family can eat only so much broccoli.

This technique will also work on many other crops, including cabbage, cauliflower, kohlrabi, beets, turnips, potatoes, tomatoes, and peas.

Take advantage of varied maturity dates by sowing a quick-growing salad crop between slower-growing vegetables like tomatoes and peppers.

CHOOSING CULTIVARS FOR CONTINUOUS HARVEST

VEGETABLE	EARLY-SEASON VARIETY	MID-SEASON VARIETY	LATE-SEASON VARIETY
Arugula	standard garden variety	'Astro'	'Sylvetta'
Beans (bush and pole)	'Provider' (bush)	'Emerite' (pole)	'Lazy Housewife' (pole)
Beets	'Early Wonder'	'Detroit Dark Red'	'Cylindra'
Broccoli	'Packman'	'Arcadia'	'Marathon'
Carrots	'Napoli' or 'Yaya'	'Scarlet Nantes'	'Napoli'
Cucumbers	'Sultan'	'Lemon'	'Armenian'
Endive	'Bianca Riccia'	'Très Fine Maraîchère'	'Batavian Full Heart'
Head lettuce	'Rouge D'Hiver'	'Ermosa'	'Winter Density'
Leaf lettuce	'Black Seeded Simpson'	'Red Sails'	'Red Salad Bowl'
Leeks	N/A (left over from winter)	'King Richard'	'Tadorna'
Mâche	'Verte de Cambrai'	'Gros Graine'	'Vit'
Mustard	'Giant Red'	'Green Wave'	'Southern Giant Curled'
Peas	'Sugar Sprint'	'Super Sugar Snap'	'Lincoln'
Potatoes	'Yukon Gold'	'Caribe'	'Rose Finn Apple'
Radishes	'D'Avignon'	'White Icicle'	'Miyashige'
Spinach	'Tyee'	'Corvair'	'Winter Giant'
Tomatoes	'Sungold'	'Costoluto Genovese'	'Brandywine'

Successful Summer Planting

IN SPRING, gardeners fret over the unexpected frosts and never-ending rains that can damage newly seeded or transplanted beds. Establishing crops for a cold-season harvest can also offer its share of challenges, as many fall and winter crops are seeded or transplanted in mid- to late summer, a time when drought and heat rule the garden.

For me, August is the prime planting season for a large variety of cool- and cold-season vegetables, yet we can go

A midsummer planting of kale provides an autumn bounty that can be enjoyed throughout winter with the help of a mini hoop tunnel.

for weeks in August without a decent rain. The resulting dry earth and high soil temperature can make it very difficult for seeds to germinate. Every species of vegetable has an ideal soil temperature for germination. If the temperature decreases below or increases above that optimum temperature range, germination rates decline and germination time increases. Lettuce, for example, will sprout well between 50 and 75°F (10–24°C), but once the soil temperature rises to 85°F (29°C), the germination rate plummets!

But don't despair: You can get around the dry soil and heat in several ways, to ensure that your summer plantings have the chance to mature into high-producing fall and winter crops.

PROVIDE SHADE

An easy way to increase the germination rates of cool-season salad crops like lettuce, mâche, and spinach is to plant them near taller plants, such as corn and tomatoes, or beneath an A-frame trellis or pole bean tepee. The cooling shade provided by the larger plants will encourage these seeds to germinate even in the heat of summer. If you happen to have a length of shade cloth lying around, you can use it to create a sheltered spot for your summer salad greens by quickly setting up a mini hoop tunnel over the garden bed and covering the ribs with the shade cloth.

Many fall and winter cold-frame vegetables also need to be planted in mid- to late summer, when the heat is unrelenting. A bit of shade can go a long way in boosting germination in hot weather and preventing newly transplanted seedlings from turning brown and crispy. I often use a piece of shade cloth on top of the open cold frame, or I toss a 3-by-6-foot piece of thin plywood on top of the frame, being careful to position it so that air can circulate but the soil is shaded. Once the seeds have germinated or the transplants have been in the ground for a few days, I start to wean the plants from the shade by allowing the cold frame to receive morning and late-afternoon sun, but I still cover it during the hottest part of the day — 10 AM to 3 PM. After a few days, the plants should be strong enough to take the sun; just remember to keep the beds irrigated.

LAY A SEEDING BARRIER

Several years ago I discovered that a simple barrier can help protect summer-seeded vegetables. It was early August and I had just planted a bed of Swiss chard, lettuce, and baby turnips for fall, as well as a package of carrots for winter. The day after I sowed the seeds, we were scheduled to go away for a few days, with no rain in the forecast. How could I keep these seeds moist and protected from the hot sun while I was away?

I gave the soil a deep watering and then covered some of the beds with a 2-inch layer of straw and the rest with some pieces of untreated scrap lumber that I raided from my hubby's woodpile in the garage. When we arrived home four days later, the carrots had just germinated beneath the lumber and the soil was still moist. When I checked on the straw-covered beds, I could see the small sprouts of the Swiss chard, lettuce, and turnips.

Remember that seeds will germinate much quicker in late summer than they do in spring, so check them often for germination if you're going to use a barrier. If you leave the barrier on too long, it can do more harm than good: the seedlings will grow tall and leggy as they stretch for the light.

POP ON A PLANT TENT

When summer skies are cloudless and the sun beats down on the garden every day, newly transplanted cool- and cold-season seedlings of kale and broccoli can quickly wilt. To prevent stress and damage after planting, water the seedlings well and then cover them with a sheet of newspaper, or a paper cone if you have newspaper-folding talents (I don't). After a day or two, or if skies turn cloudy, remove the covering and the plant should be ready to take the sun.

WATER WELL

Okay, this should be obvious, but it's so important that it's worth mentioning. The soil of newly seeded or transplanted garden beds dries out faster in the summer than it does in spring, when rain is more plentiful. Therefore, you'll need to get out the hose to keep the soil moist until your seeds germinate or the transplants start to put out new growth. Typically, I water my newly planted summer beds every day or two for a few weeks, unless we've had a good supply of rain. Remember to water deeply, to encourage good root systems.

To help ensure good germination and growth of cool- and cold-season crops during a warm autumn, water beds frequently.

MULCH IT

Once you've nestled in your baby kale, broccoli, and kohlrabi transplants for fall and winter crops, give the soil a deep watering (or transplant on a rainy day) and apply a thick layer of straw or shredded leaves to the beds. This will help prevent moisture loss from both the soil and the plants, as well as suppress weeds.

Interplanting

Interplanting is another technique that is used in intensive gardening, and it's a great way to get more out of your space without expanding your current garden. Interplanting is closely related to companion planting, which pairs up two or more plants for a mutually beneficial purpose, such as attracting beneficial insects and pollinators or deterring pests. Interplanting, on the other hand, is simply combining two or more types of vegetables in the same garden bed at the same time in order to maximize the growing area.

The goal of interplanting isn't to have numerous types of vegetables competing for the same space, light, moisture, and nutrients. Rather, you should combine plants with different maturity dates, growth patterns, and growing requirements. For example, once my broccoli transplants are set out in the garden in mid-spring, I sprinkle my favorite mix of baby lettuce seed on the empty expanse of soil between and around the small seedlings. By the time the broccoli needs the space, the lettuce has long since been harvested. Plus, the lettuce creates a living mulch that helps prevent weed growth around the broccoli and shields the soil on hot days, thereby minimizing moisture evaporation.

A little thought before you plant will help you get the most out of your interplanting efforts. For the best results, it helps to know maturity dates, plant shapes (tall, short,

Plants that belong to the same family usually do not make good planting partners. Not only are they likely to compete for the same nutrients, but they may also attract the same pests, increasing the chances of an infestation.

Interplanting 'Black Seeded Simpson' lettuce among my spring cabbages allows me to harvest more from my space. Plus, the vibrant green lettuce suppresses weeds and adds welcome color to the early garden.

spreading, upright), preferred season of growth (cool, warm, or cold), and cultivation information (light, water, and nutrient needs).

Successful interplanting also requires good, fertile soil. In order to coax more than one vegetable from the same patch of soil, you must ensure that your soil is well amended with compost or aged manure. If fertility is a problem, also add some granular organic fertilizer.

Interplanting also increases the biodiversity of your garden. This, in turn, can attract both pollinating and beneficial insects, which will help increase yields and keep any pest populations under control. The flowers of certain plants, like parsley, dill, coriander, fennel, sweet alyssum, carrots, and parsnips, are known for their ability to lure beneficial insects. I also like to include a range of vegetables, herbs, and annuals with showy blossoms to entice pollinating bees and wasps. Some of my favorites to plant in the vegetable patch are sunflowers, zinnias, cosmos, squash, cucumbers, sage, marjoram, lavender, and basil. See the chart on page 234 for a convenient interplanting guide.

Benefits of Interplanting

- Maximizes garden space
- Minimizes weeds
- Can help foil pests by disguising their favorite host plants
- Creates visual interest
- Attracts pollinators and beneficial insects to your garden

By the time these 'Sungold' tomatoes are ready to harvest, the 'Outredgeous' lettuce will have been harvested, thus providing the tomatoes space to sprawl.

Here are the three interplanting systems I use in my garden.

Staggered Maturity

Planting crops that mature at different times is the easiest way to practice interplanting. Just pick two types of crops with different maturity dates — the further apart, the better. Certain vegetables are quick growing and are considered short-season crops; others need more time to mature and are long-season crops. By combining these two different types of veggies in one space (like my broccoli and lettuce), you'll be able to harvest two crops from the same garden bed. If you waited to succession-plant that bed, you would need to delay planting the lettuce until the broccoli was harvested. Not very efficient.

A classic interplanting combination is pairing carrots with radishes. Both are planted at the same time — you can even mix the seed together — and because the radishes are so quick to germinate (often in just 2 or 3 days), they mark the row for the slower-growing carrots. Then, when the radishes are harvested, 3 to 4 weeks later, they loosen and aerate the soil, making room for the slower-maturing carrots.

Plant Shape

Another way to combine plants in the same space is to choose those with different forms, or "architecture."

Tall plants can be mixed with short plants, upright with spreading, and aboveground with belowground (root). I like to plants beets between my onions, radishes between my tomatoes (and just about everywhere else), and lettuce at the base of my corn. Corn and lettuce are also a great combo for a midsummer garden, when the soaring temperatures can leave lettuce weak and wilted in a matter of minutes. The corn will provide some shelter from the sun, which the lettuce appreciates.

Cultural Needs

Crops can also be paired with vegetables that have different cultivation requirements. For example, light feeders can be planted with heavy feeders and full sun lovers with those that prefer partial shade. Typically, it is the leafy vegetables that are the most shade tolerant, although certain root crops are also moderately tolerant of partial sun. Among those crops that can withstand some shading are beets, arugula, lettuce, Swiss chard, mustard, kale, spinach, kohlrabi, endive, and turnip. Plant them beside taller vegetables like pole beans, peas, corn, and tomatoes.

You can also combine light feeders — including beans, turnips, onions, and beets — with heavier feeders: for example, broccoli and corn. Certain crops, like beans and peas, can even "fix" nitrogen from the air, enriching the soil around them. This ability makes them perfect for nitrogen-greedy crops like greens, brassicas, and corn.

FAVORITE COMBINATIONS FOR INTERPLANTING

VEGETABLE	SUGGESTED LOCATION
ARUGULA	between tomatoes under pole beans or trellised cucumbers
BASIL	between tomatoes
BUSH BEANS	between tomatoes, peppers, or eggplant
BEETS	between brassicas (broccoli, Brussels sprouts, cabbage, cauliflower), onions, leeks, or zucchini
CARROTS	between bush beans, leeks, or tomatoes
CILANTRO	between leeks
LETTUCE	under corn, pole beans, or tomatoes; between celery, celeriac, leeks, or brassicas
ONIONS	between cabbage plants (or any other member of the brassica family)
PARSLEY	between tomatoes
RADISHES	everywhere (they're said to help repel pests when planted with cucumbers or squash)
SPINACH	under pole beans or trellised cucumbers and between leeks, turnips, and brassicas
WINTER SQUASH	under corn